Baseball For Building Boys To Men

Rick Saggese, XFS, CSAC

ISBN: 978-0-9916026-5-0

DEDICATION

<u>Rick Saggese, Jr.</u>

To my dad, Rick Saggese, Sr, who always provided by the opportunity to succeed if it was through training aids or moving our family from Massachusetts to Florida so I could have more opportunities to reach my baseball goals. He always made sure I had the proper resources so I could pursue my dreams of becoming the best baseball player that I could. I am forever grateful for the time and bond we shared, even though it was cut short, the 16 years we had was more special than many have in a lifetime.

<u>Cecile Saggese</u>

Rick Saggese, Sr was a dedicated to baseball and helping kids that wanted to learn and better their skills. It didn't matter what level they were. If at any time he felt they were wasting his time, that was the end. Rick Sr always sought new learning tools to better the strength and psychological part of baseball and worked endlessly with Rick Jr. At times he was hard on his son, but Rick Jr. has the right temperament and always took everything in stride. All for the love of the game. Wife of 24 years. You will never be forgotten I will always love you.

<u>Bob Saggese</u>

My brother was someone that was there for me every step of the way. Baseball was his life along with his family. He did what he thought was best in everything he did-all the way or no way. His mentorship was second to none. His dreams and vision for what he did was always in his sight. His motivation was in him all the time-to succeed and be the best at what you did. As a younger brother I always looked up to him- he was my DREAM of what I wanted to be and do with my life. He may be gone but his legacy will always live with me in my heart- love you brother!

TABLE OF CONTENTS

Title Page
Copyright
Dedication
Table Of Contents
Wisdom Index Cards
Acknowledgements

YOU MUST HAVE . . .

PATIENCE } TO WAIT FOR YOUR PITCH.

AND

DISCIPLINE } TO RESPOND CORRECTLY.

PATIENCE AND DISCIPLINE MAKE GREAT HITTERS IN THE MAJORS.

The Splendid Splinter   The Iron Horse   The Hitman   ARIBA   The K   MR. K   WILL   The Thrill   The Bambino

---

THREE RULES TO HIT BY

* ONLY POWER STIKES ON 1ST PITCH

① GET A GOOD BALL TO HIT.
(BE PATIENT — SWING ONLY AT STIKES- KNOW YOUR STRIKE ZONE.)

② PROPER THINKING.
(KNOW THE PITCHER — FIGURE WHAT HE MIGHT TRY TO DO.)

③ BE QUICK WITH THE BAT.
(BE CONFIDENT IN YOUR HITTING ABILITY- SWING SMOOTHLY AND SWIFTLY.)

-T. WILLIAMS

These were index cards my dad wrote and posted in our cellar where I trained year round. He always was reading and learning different aspects of the game and regularly posted these to help me become a better ball player.

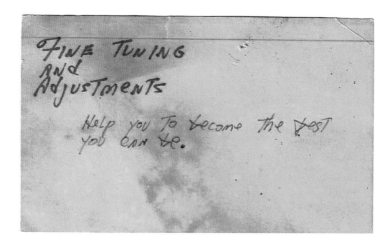

SCOUTS LOOK FOR:
(LEFT-handed Hitter)

1. From Behind The plate:
   the batter strides Toward The pitcher.

2. From Third base:
   the batter keeps his hands back
   when striding.

3. From First base:
   the batter's front shoulder stays
   closed — slightly down & In.

4. The batter has quick hands & excellent bat speed.

FINE TUNING
AND
Adjustments

Help you To become the best
you can be.

Even if it was a short comment he never forgot to
write it down for me to read.

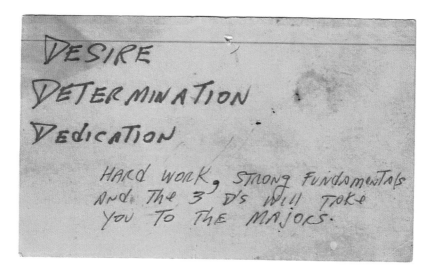

The 3 D's were talked about a lot as this was the foundation of our belief system. My dad always believed that looking like a ball player had an effect on the way you played the game.

TO BE A GREAT HITTER
BE PATIENT. . .
GET your pitch
TO HIT. . .
MAKE THE pitcher
Throw Your pitch !!!

Written the morning of my dad's accident he was
providing guidance all the way to the end.

ACKNOWLEDGMENTS

<u>Rick Saggese, Jr</u>

I want to thank my mom (Cecile) and dad (Rick, Sr.), who were always there for me during the peaks and valleys during my career. They were the reason I got the opportunity to have the success that I did and they are the main reason why I can help so many players and people today.

Thank you to my wife, Lisa, for giving me the support and opportunity for allowing me to do what I'm passionate about for a living.

 Thank you to my sister, Tammy and her husband John for allowing and trusting in me to help their son, Seth, develop his leadership and baseball skills.

I would like to thank every coach and manager I ever had the opportunity to play for:

<u>Jim Arnold</u>: My Little League World Series team coach in Andover, Massachusetts.

<u>Rick Harrison</u>: My pony league Andover Gold coach in Andover, Massachusetts.

<u>Dave Bettencourt</u>: Baseball Coach who taught me much in Andover, Massachusetts.

<u>Peter Reppucci</u>: An angel that was sent after my father passed who took me under his wing like a step dad in Naples, Florida.

<u>Bob Smith</u>: My High School head coach who helped guide me to All State and All American honors at Barron Collier in Naples, Florida.

<u>Bill Wolf:</u> My High School coach at Barron Collier in Naples, Florida who helped me after my father passed.

Johnny Rodriguez: My batting coach at the University of Miami for all the help during my collegiate career.

Turtle Thomas: The recruiter who recruited me which gave me the opportunity to play my college baseball at the University of Miami in Coral Gables, Florida.

Jim Morris: My College coach who gave me the opportunity to become a College All American at the University of Miami in Coral Gables, Florida.

Thank you to Gary Monahan, a past client at Think Outside The Diamond Sports Performance & Fitness for his assistance in daily operations as well as helping with our book photos.

CHAPTER 1- PRE GAME

"If it's going to be it's up to me." -Brian Tracy

My father was the wind beneath my wings throughout the course of my childhood. He lead by example, showed me what it took to be successful and showed me how to chase a dream. He provided me with everything he possibly could have to ensure my success; and my thanks are never ending.

As I grew older, our bond grew inseparable. Every morning he would go for a run, I would bike alongside him. He opened a bakery when we lived in Reading, Massachusetts, and I would work beside him after school. We collected baseball cards incessantly throughout my childhood. As my love for the game of baseball took off, our relationship grew even stronger.

I played a handful of sports growing up: football, baseball, hockey, soccer and basketball. By the time I was ten years old, I knew baseball was the sport in which I wanted to pursue. It wasn't just for fun, and it wasn't just a hobby. I grew extremely passionate towards the game, and when my dad realized just how serious I was about it, he relentlessly provided me with the tools for success. He was more than willing to wholeheartedly support my dream.

I was still in elementary school when my dad built a training facility in the cellar of our home. I trained five days a week, rain or shine. He had cut a tire in half for me to swing into, building up my hand and wrist strength. There were batting tees, mirrors for me to evaluate my stance in, and plyometric boxes in the cellar with me. My father had provided me with all of the equipment I needed to become a better player. He would research techniques and training methods often; he was as devoted to my success as I was.

Soon enough, I had outgrown the training facility in the cellar, and so, my father hired a crew to install a batting cage into our backyard. My dad was that kind of person: if he chose to do something, he would do it to the absolute best of his ability. If he was going to support my dream, he was going to do so wholeheartedly. He coached my team at Andover Little League to several victories when I was ten and eleven years old.

During the summer of 1988, our All-star team came together as we worked towards a common goal: the Little League World Series. Winning the state tournament in Massachusetts, we headed to Bristol, Connecticut, for regionals. We took on Delaware, and by the sixth inning, the game was tied at six. Fortunately for me, it seemed as though extra innings brought luck. We were in the ninth inning with the bases loaded as I stepped into the batter's box. At this very moment, all my hard work had paid off: I sent the ball over the fence and my team to victory. My first official grand slam would be one that brought my team and I to the Little League World Series, and one that I would never forget.

We had the time of our lives as twelve-year-old boys, playing on the biggest stage we ever had during the race to the Little League World Series in Pennsylvania. We lost our first game to Texas, and were placed in the loser's bracket. The following game, I pitched as we claimed our first victory against Panama. Unfortunately, we dropped our third and last game to Saudi Arabia, and were therefore not one of the eight teams to make it to the finals. Though the tournament didn't go ideally in our favor, it was an experience of a lifetime.

When we returned back home from Pennsylvania, we were regarded as hometown baseball stars: the whole town threw a party, we paraded down the streets in the beds of pickup trucks as people honked their horns and cheered for us. I had pitched for the team at this time, but my focus soon became hitting. The word in baseball is, "If you can hit, you'll always find a place to play."

I played for a few more years in Andover when

my parents revealed their consideration of moving to
Florida. My parents knew I had the determination and
dedication it would take to make it far in baseball,
and to enhance my training, they wished to move our
family to Naples, Florida, therefore providing me
with the opportunity to train year round. During a
trip to Naples, we went to meet with Barron Collier
High School's varsity baseball coach, Bob Smith; we
waited for him in the parking lot as we realized time
was being wasted. My dad popped open the trunk of the
rental car and tossed me balls to hit into it. Coach
Smith saw my swing and said, "I love your swing! You
can start as a freshman!" And so, I went to Barron
Collier High School, playing first base as a
freshman; the first freshman to start on varsity in
the school's history.

Upon moving to Florida, my father became more
than a parent to me. He became my mentor, my coach,
and my best friend. He always expressed how proud of
me he was, and showed me the kind of person I wish to
be.

Before a game against Miami Westminster
Christian School, during my sophomore year at Barron
Collier, my dad offered to come out early for my
teammates and I to hold batting practice. This game
would be a tough one, as Miami Westminster Christian
had a reputation for creating all-stars, like Alex
Rodriguez and Doug Mientkiewicz who were both on that
team in 1992. We were facing a left-handed pitcher
with a dominating curveball; my father was left-
handed, so was an asset to our batting practice. If
we could beat such a formidable team, we would be
nationally recognized.

Everyone took their turn in the cage. Once I
finished batting, I took the field, and within
minutes heard unnerving shouts from the batting
cages.

A batter had hit a line drive, which struck my
dad in the head. As he bent down to grab another
ball, insisting he was alright, he fell to the
ground. Paramedics arrived, and told us he would be

okay; nevertheless, we stood there horrified, overwhelmed in pure fear, as they continued to perform CPR, and it continued to prevail ineffective.

It was on March 19, 1992, that my father passed. The ball that hit him caused an undetected aneurysm in his head to rupture. We played the game against Miami Westminster Christian in his honor, as we did every other game that season. My family was devastated; he was the glue that held our family together. My team was devastated as well; that day was one that several of my teammates and myself included could never put a word on, the devastation was simply indescribable. Losing my father is something I will never get over. He was, and continues to be, the most selfless person I have ever met. If he thought a player had a single ounce of talent, he would maximize it, whether it be with a simple compliment or a training technique he thought they should try.

I had never been more motivated to "make it" in baseball. I told my high school coach, Bob Smith, who sat beside me that day in the emergency room, "You know Coach, I'm gonna make it to the big leagues someday. I'm gonna do it for my dad." I wrote on a baseball to place in his casket, "Everything I'm going to accomplish is for you."

The following season, universities began to recruit me. Scouts from small schools often came to practices unannounced, whereas more well-known schools such as the University of Miami, Stetson and Clemson University made their interest in me blatant. Despite my knee injury during my junior year, I persevered, rehabbing my way back onto the field for my final season as a Barron Collier Cougar.

I ended up at the University of Miami on a baseball scholarship. In my eyes, all I had to do was accept college life, get by academically, and then get drafted.

Like most things in life, this didn't go as planned. I played well at the University of Miami, and am ever grateful for the time I spent there.

During the summers of my sophomore and junior year at Miami, I headed back up north and played in the Cape Cod Collegiate Baseball League, and started for the Hyannis Mets. Upon playing there, I was lucky enough to play alongside past former major-leaguers, such as Eric Hinske, Eric Byrnes, and JJ Putz. During these summers, I lived in Massachusetts with a teammate from Miami and a host family.

Throughout my time at the University of Miami, I accumulated a .302 batting average, with 21 home runs and 101 RBIs. I was fortunate to play in three College World Series, and became a Collegiate All American my freshman year. That same year, we played LSU in the 1996 National Championship, falling behind by one run as Warren Morris hit a walk off, two run homerun. The final score was 9-8, LSU, and the game is still regarded as one of the most memorable in College World Series history. However, after three seasons and a series of knee injuries, I lost my scholarship. Rarely playing in perfect health, I was not as valuable as a designated hitter or first baseman as I once was. I finished by collegiate baseball career at Florida International University where we won the Sunbelt Conference Championship and I finally got a ring.

I went back to Naples with a frustrated, deflated mind, and two knees that gave up the fight way too soon. I had never seriously considered what I would do in life if baseball didn't work out for me, as I had always doubtlessly assumed it would. I moonlighted as a substitute teacher, held day jobs here and there, and took courses. Nonetheless, baseball continued to remain a thought in the back of my mind.

Jobs came and went, and I began to study towards my second degree as a teacher. I worked as a physical education teacher for a period of time, and began training kids in certain aspects of the game of baseball in the afternoon. On the weekends, after school, and any extra second I had, I continued to learn about fitness, nutrition, and baseball. I was optimistic that the future would bring good fortune, as I hoped to someday open my own baseball training facility.

My passion for the game runs deep, and I believe this is why I was lead back to the game. I began to train more and *more* players. I decided to launch my own website as I assisted high school coaches with speed and agility training during summers, and wished to aid athletes of all types. I had been training athletes since 2000, but my goal was to open my own training facility. With time, this dream became reality, as I opened up an indoor facility in Naples in 2012. Every day, I am granted my wish to mentor, train, and coach athletes of all kinds, as well as individuals of all ages aiming to pursue a healthier, more active lifestyle.

My father was the greatest mentor I have ever had, as he relayed all of his knowledge, in all aspects of life and the game of baseball, to me. As I am now presented, each and every day, with the opportunity to mentor and coach athletes of all sorts, I feel as though this is what I was meant to do, and I feel as though I have built a life for myself that my father would be extremely proud of.

CHAPTER 2- POWER OF A POSITIVE BELIEF SYSTEM

"If you believe, you will achieve."-Rick Saggese, Jr.

Belief is defined as trust or confidence in someone or something. Believing in yourself has unprecedented value in both life and the game of baseball.

After my father passed, my mother relentlessly aimed to instill a positive belief system into my head. The hard times we endured lead me, as well as my mother, to the realization that negativity drags a person down, and illustrated how impactful positivity is regarding long-term success.

The power of the positive belief system that was instilled in me is indescribable; I aim to instill the same belief system into each and every one of my athletes right off the bat. Each new client I speak with, I ask the same question, "Who do you feel is a great athlete?" More times than not, they reply with a Major League Baseball player in whom they admire. Starting here, I make my first attempt to alter an athlete's mindset. For an athlete to be successful at any age, they must believe that they are great at what they do; I wish to not only leave each athlete I train with this mentality, but also elucidate to them why confidence and positivity are so vital to the game.

During training, I typically will ask performance-related questions such as, "Who wants to be at the plate with the game on the line?" and, "What makes you a champion?" Throughout the course of a session, I will question and praise athletes in order to aid in the building of their positive belief system.

I utilize a self-evaluation worksheet as I see needed. Players with low self-esteem and a lack of confidence complete this, answering yes or no questions such as, "I am talented enough to participate at the level of competition I desire," and open-ended questions like, "My main reasons for participating in sports are…" By completing this worksheet, players with a poor mindset are able to jot down their thoughts regarding the topic, and move forward from there.

Training above the neck is crucial; an athlete can have all of the physical talent in the world, but if they don't have the right mindset, they will only go so far. With a positive mindset and belief system instilled, athletes train themselves to expect success rather than failure, and to believe in themselves and their capabilities. Talent can take an athlete places, but only so many; Confidence and positivity opens the door completely, leaving players with no limits to their success.

Standing in the batter's box, there is no room in an athlete's mind for doubt. There is a pitch to recognize, a bat to swing, and a job to be done. Looking for reasons to doubt yourself in the game of baseball, as well as life, is the equivalent to looking for a bucket of curveballs. Standing in the batter's box, hands should be quick and a mind should be quiet, and therefore not abound with self-doubt. In regards to positive reinforcement, I always tell my athletes, "We live in a negative world, you have to be positive, and you have to do it for yourself." To be a consistent, successful hitter, an athlete must have the firm belief system set: they must truly believe that they are a consistent, successful hitter.

In the game of baseball especially, a positive belief system is crucial: players fail more than they succeed. In 2016, the Major League had an overall batting average of .255. With this said, the average professional baseball player is not getting a hit 74.5% of the time. Baseball is considered the most self-esteem destructing sport for this reason, expanding the need for a positive belief system.

Several young athletes lack a strong

understanding of the correlation between the process and results. The process is in the hands of the athlete, whereas the results are not. I encourage players to focus on the "controllables," and therefore, the process, their health, their mindset, and everything else in their control.

From a group perspective, an athlete's positive, confident attitude becomes contagious. Watching thousands, and being a part of hundreds, of baseball games, it has become easy to see who emerges as a leader on the team; I see a pattern repeating in these regards, as it is typically the athlete who is the most positive, and has the most faith in their own abilities. A single positive mindset can completely alter the mindset of an entire team.

In order to fulfill this positive belief system, goals must be set. I often have athletes of all ages set long term and short term goals, as well as aid them in creating their plan to achieve this goal, in order to make it a reality. A goal is nothing but a thought, unless there is a plan behind it. I remind my athletes often nonetheless, that in order for goals to become reality, one must be persistent, consistent, and patient. All-stars are not made overnight. Before bed, I encourage players to tell themselves, "I am strong, focused, and play with total confidence."

A key to creating the proper mindset is incorporating physical activity before each pitch, regardless of offense or defense. For example, as a hitter, one may redo the Velcro on their batting gloves. Directly after, players should breathe: inhaling through their nose, and exhaling through their mouth. This physical activity and breathing technique provides the athlete a chance to release any tension they may have at the moment, allowing them to recognize, release, and regroup. Several high-level players choose to chew gum as they play for the same reason.

Bright athletes sabotage their performance by over thinking, usually relating back to personal, perfectionist tendencies. Baseball is not a game of perfection whatsoever, and mistakes must be shaken off. Players must trust their athletic abilities and avoid a high-strung mindset. To quiet an athlete's mind, they must understand that practice is over at the start of competition. Mechanics should not be practiced during competition; instead, they should have confidence in what they have already learned. Also during competition, an athlete shouldn't aim to fix what might not be broken. When a mistake is made, athletes with perfectionist tendencies try to analyze what went wrong; in a game especially, they should simply move onto the next pitch instead.

Simplifying cues regarding performance for athletes who overthink has a tremendous impact, especially in the batter's box. Players should have the saying, "See the ball, hit the ball," on their mind when they're at bat, and avoid thinking about each and every tip their coach has given them.

In a game that is 90% mental, a player's mindset and belief system play the biggest factors in their success. As a trainer and mentor, I focus on developing players just as much mentally, as I do physically. I see several athletes who completely transform their attitude towards the game, and positively transform their performance simultaneously.

CHAPTER 3- STYLES OF TEACHING

"A coach will impact more young people in a year than the average person does in a lifetime." -Billy Graham

The impact a coach has on an athlete, whether it be positive or negative, could mean the difference between a good player and a great player. Anything and everything that I teach to my athletes, I have a reason for. I aim to fulfill my role as a coach, mentor, and teacher in its fullest potential, ensuring my players with as much success as they're willing to work for. While I remind players of their talent and capabilities, I refuse to neither praise them nor choose not to point out their mistakes. More often than not, I see coaches lack a skill for teaching players. It's usually assumed that all coaches do nothing more than transfer information and knowledge about the game. I wish to train and mentor athletes, teaching them as much as possible about the game, implementing a steady mindset towards the game, and aiding them on their road to success, rather than just simply coaching them; I aim to have an ongoing, interactive relationship with my players, avoiding a one-way line of communication.

By teaching players, I am giving them the opportunity to learn and develop, and increasing the chances that they are enjoying the game, and will continue to in the long run. By solely coaching players, this enjoyment factor is incredibly weakened, along with the development factor. In this situation, success is typically limited for the athlete.

I have been around coaches since the first time I stepped on a baseball field in Andover. Even today, I make an effort to speak with several coaches. I have recognized a few, distinct types of coaches: those who yell incessantly, those who are far too quiet, those who are negative, and those who are positive.

Coaches who are always yelling are at a loss; their players inevitably begin to tune them out, resulting in minimum improvement. The respect the athlete has towards the coach is short-term, if not absent, and the team is engaged in an atmosphere of intimidation and fear. Also at a loss are coaches who adapt a negative approach to the game. In this situation, players begin to fear failure and mistakes, and slowly become less enthusiastic towards the game. Negative coaches put such intense pressure on their players that they have a hard time understanding the concept that baseball is a game of mistakes and that failure is inevitable.

The most laidback approach to coaching is taken by those who are quiet. While at times a quiet coach is ideal, they may not be instructing players to the fullest extent. Quiet coaches will typically fail to effectively communicate with their players, and therefore not teach players all they wish to learn.

These evaluations are supplements to my belief that a positive approach to coaching is the most beneficial for the player. Players remain engaged in the game and enthusiastic towards improvement, but are not being cheated out of instruction. Positive reinforcement plays a significant role in player's mentality towards the game; an interactive relationship is formed between the athlete and the coaches, and there is an increase of participation due to the environment created.

Science aims to back up the "art of coaching." One must understand a 'coaching cue': a bit of task-oriented information that will aim to teach an athlete how to perform a skill. Among coaching cues are external, internal, and normal cues.

Internal cues lead athletes to focus their attention on body movements. For example, in relation to sprinting, an internal cue may sound something like, "Keep your chest up tall." Internal cues have a negative connotation because they are believed to disrupt the body's movement and control as an athlete aims to consciously organize their body. Normal cues refer to the absence of instruction from a coach, and are therefore the athlete's point of focus with no cue at all.

External cues have been scientifically proven to be the most beneficial, and I therefore utilize them in my training sessions. With external cues, athletes focus on the movement outcome associated with the skill they're performing. These are favored cues because they reduce the conscious interference caused by internal cues and cause the athlete to be more concerned with the outcome than the internal actions needed.

Along with external cues, I make a conscious effort to push chronic, rather than acute learning onto my athletes. Acute learning refers to temporary, short-term improvement, and can be the result of poor coaching. If an athlete is unable to reproduce their skill in a game a month later, their improvement was temporary, and their learning was acute. Chronic learning is the complete opposite, and refers to permanent improvement. With chronic learning, players' minds become embedded with the information snippets they need to perform a skill correctly, in a way they won't forget. For example, everything an athlete does on a baseball field during a game should be natural, and the athlete should be able to "do it in their sleep." If this is the case, these skills are permanent in their mind, and won't be lost anytime soon.

It is vital for coaches to get a sense of how each individual learns best, whether it be through listening, seeing, or doing. It should, however, not be misunderstood that all learners will need to try skills for themselves; learning styles solely suggest in which method an athlete would learn best.

Auditory learners value sounds, words, and discussions: coaches should put attention towards auditory performance cues, and utilize in-depth verbal descriptions of skills. Some coaches have chosen to tape record descriptions simply for auditory learners; they're the most likely to go back and listen to it over and over again, as they value repetition. While some coaches hate repeating the same simple, command incessantly, it may be the most beneficial for these types of learners. Players of this learning style are quick to pick up slight changes in a person's tone of voice, and therefore better understand their coach's expectations.

Visual learners acquire knowledge primarily through their visual acuity. They would prefer to see a skill demonstrated, and utilize visual aids often. Typically, these athletes appreciate watching film and analyzing charts. While coaching a visual learner, coaches should use keywords such as, 'imagine' and, 'focus.' For learners of this style, I suggest considering using a "sign of success": visual reminders of what you have learned. An example would be writing, "Controlled violence," on the lid of their hat; this may act as a reminder to whip the bat through the zone, utilizing your hips.

Athletes that need to do or feel in order to learn best are referred to as kinesthetic learners. These athletes can watch a demonstration of a skill and listen to a description, but may still feel as though they are missing something: they need to do it themselves, and gain a feel for the movement as a whole. Through this, athletes will usually develop a "frame" of how the movement or skill should feel. They value repetition, similar to auditory learners. The kinesthetic learning style is most common among athletes, and they typically have exceptional hand-eye coordination. While training, athletes of this learning style should avoid sitting, even if they're simply talking to their coach. Coaches should aim to make suggestions and comments regarding performance as the athlete is performing.

With each athlete I train, I make a conscious effort to learn his or her personality. I believe it is absolutely vital to adjust ways of teaching in regards to the individual being taught. Whether it be the tone of voice or the intensity of the session, I aim to adapt to each player I train; some players need to learn to hustle, others need to learn to relax. I take pride in providing each athlete with his or her own unique training experience.

Crucial to a player's value is their ability to be coached. I often explain to my athletes that talent, supplemented with the ability to be coached leads to value. Several coaches at higher levels would choose a slightly less talented individual that is coachable over a talented player with no desire to be coached or taught; if a player isn't coachable, their talent is nearly useless.

No coach is the same; each will have their strengths and weaknesses. Ultimately, I aim to play the role of who an athlete needs as their coach, whether it be someone to get under their skin and make them work, or someone to aid them in adapting a positive mindset. Regardless, I choose to take a positive approach to coaching in order to fulfill my role in its highest capacity as a coach and teacher.

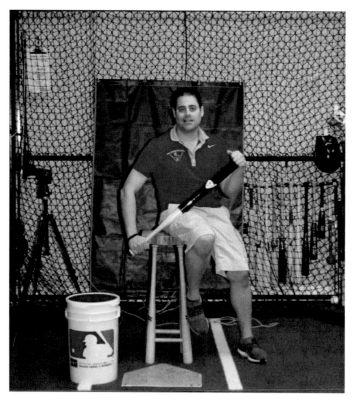

CHAPTER 4-BEING A WELL ROUNDED PLAYER

"It's hard to beat a person who never gives up." - Babe Ruth

For training purposes, I have broken down the aspects of baseball for my clients. The five aspects, in my eyes, are skill set, mentality, flexibility, strength, and visual acuity. All five aspects are connected; players are at the top of their game when their skill set, mentality, flexibility, strength, and visual acuity are maximized to their fullest potential. In a typical session with an athlete, I aim to tap into three of the five aspects. Versatility is underestimated in not only the game of baseball, but in nearly all sports, and should be held to a higher value; therefore, you should work on all aspects of the game.

A player's skill set is their ability to throw, hit, bunt, play the infield and outfield, run the bases, and pitch. I believe that players should aim to be a multi-dimensional player, rather than just a shortstop, or just a first baseman. As a multi-dimensional player, athletes should have a wide range of skill set and be able to play anywhere in the field comfortably and with confidence. Skill set takes much time and commitment; you want these varies skills to become "muscle memory." Nonetheless, I greatly stress the importance of quality over quantity while training these specific skill sets.

The lack of patience kids possess in today's world isn't going to help them in this situation, as they fail to fully commit to the process. I usually assign my clients "homework" so that they're able to get in numerous reps; practicing a new skill during a session and then not practicing for a week after that will not be beneficial. Without the proper skill set, a player is considered just an "athlete", and not a baseball player.

The mental aspect of the game is partially up to the athlete: they must have confidence in their abilities, and rely on a positive mindset at all times. In order to do my part as a player's coach and mentor, I teach them specifics on how to train their mind to turn negatives into positives and aid them in setting short and long term goals, as well as adopting a positive belief system. Players usually look at a situation as what they did wrong or what they did right. On the other hand, I teach players to look at both: recognizing what was done wrong in necessary, as this will lead them to see room for improvement and growth. Recognizing what was done well allows players to remain in a positive mindset. Performance related questions and encouragement are also key elements in my training sessions, as they are huge factors in allowing a player to develop this mindset. Getting players to buy into this thinking process is the most difficult thing I face as a trainer and mentor. Players are usually committed to fixing their physical game, but don't realize the commitment it takes to repair their mental game. Mental toughness makes or breaks players, and is truly as important as physical training is.

As far as strength is concerned, a player should consider the following: Are your joints strong enough to handle the load you are putting on them? Are you strong enough to remain healthy and injury-free throughout your season?
Not only does strength maximize the power output of a player's skill set, but it also protects athletes from injuries and affects speed, agility, power, mobility, and explosiveness - all key abilities on the field.

A weak upper back is a ball player's worst

nightmare: throwing puts so much stress on the shoulder and is so unnatural that a weak upper back can eventually lead to a blocked rotation of their shoulder joint. With blocked rotation, the extra motion created by throwing is inevitably transferred down to the elbow joint; this extreme amount of stress on the elbow is what leads to players' need for Tommy John's surgery, and possibly to the end of their baseball career. Elbow injuries can also be caused by a lack of arm strength.

The best hitters generate an exceptional amount of power from their forearms and wrists. With strong forearms and wrists, they have increased bat control, allowing them to whip their bat through the zone.

In order to increase bat speed, players should also consider strengthening their chest muscles. These muscles also connect to the shoulder and upper back muscles; the stronger they are, the lesser the chances are for injury.

A strong core allows for players to adapt an explosive manner of play, and also increases their balance, body control, and movement efficiency, as well as allow for powerful output to their limbs. The core is the base of all movement, which should be reason enough to choose to develop a strong one.

Hip extension is the source of a significant amount of athletic power in general, and the hamstrings and glutes are responsible for this function. Strong hamstrings and glutes allow players to create power at the plate, quickly sprint, push off the mound, and accelerate faster. In the same conversation are players' calves, as they're contributors to the same movements. Ultimately, strong legs allow players to quickly move and play explosively.

Flexibility is overlooked in the game of baseball. Player's range of motion is paramount to their execution of moving efficiently and with power simultaneously. Flexible athletes are at less of a risk for injury, as their bodies are better prepared for the repetitive stress baseball puts on them.

Muscle imbalances can be avoided by flexibility, lessening the chances for athletes to eventually pull their joint out of alignment. ⬚Muscle imbalances are unfortunately common for baseball players, as you throw with the same arm, plant the same foot, and run in the same direction. For this reason, it's important to train both arms and both legs the same. Flexible hips are paramount in baseball, as you will use them to drive the ball at the plate, to explode out of the catcher's position, and drive off the mound. Tight hips in athletes can not only affect their performance negatively, but also lead to lower back issues. Neck muscles, shoulders, elbows, and wrists are put under lots of stress, as the same few motions are repeated: tracking fly balls, throwing with the same arm, and hitting. A flexible core is valued in regards to the rotational movement executed when hitting, and limber legs allow for players to more efficiently change directions and sprint.

Trainers should look to see the asymmetry between shoulders: their asymmetry is vital for lasting shoulder and joint health. Baseball, along with a handful of other sports, put tons of stress on one arm, the throwing arm. If players fail to train their non-throwing arm, the joints will adopt impingements. For this reason, players and coaches should do everything in their power to balance the two. Often times, the throwing shoulder is elevated in comparison to the non-throwing shoulder; this distortion can be caused by tight traps and/or scapular muscles, which are a result of constantly throwing with the same arm. In certain situations, I recommend that clients go to chiropractors on a regular basis in order to ensure that these imbalances are being taken care of properly before any injuries occur.

With the extreme amount of stress high-level players place on their bodies, there is an exceptional amount of room for injury; nonetheless, the risk can be largely reduced by implementing stretching into workouts and practices.

The final aspect of being a well-rounded player is visual acuity. Elite players should be able to track a moving object, a pitch in particular, and process information quickly. This aspect is typically overlooked, but needs training, just as the physical and mental aspects of baseball do. At the beginning of sessions, I have several of my players utilize technology to identify pitches and tendencies in pitchers. I also utilize drills where I have players identify the absence or presence of a number written on a tennis ball that I toss to them, followed by the batter trying to hit the same ball.

In the same conversation is concentration and focus. Regarding focus, I utilize a visual trainer and training aids such as strobe training glasses, which distorts hitters' visions, and leaves their central nervous system to process the information, allowing the athlete to perform the skill with the external nervous system and utilize their limbs. Also aiming to improve players' focus and concentration, I have them catch flying cards, forcing them to use their hand-eye coordination.

When athletes train frequently, they are simulating their central nervous system, which is what they rely on while executing skills; this is more commonly known as muscle memory. Athletes often forget how important practice is: during competition, however, players typically don't think about what they're doing, they just do it. This is the result of innumerable hours of practice, training the same muscles to execute a skill in a certain way. The process isn't an easy one; athletes have the opportunity to point to a thousand reasons to quit along the way, yet those who find the reason to continue relentless training and genuinely trust in the process come out on top.

At the end of the day, all players have their flaws, and none will ever be perfect in each and every aspect. Nonetheless, I encourage players to train relentlessly to improve on all five aspects of the game. The more versatile a player becomes, the

stronger they get, the faster and the more flexible
they become, they maximize their potential as a
baseball player more and more.

CHAPTER 5-DEVELOPMENT VS COMPETITION

"It ain't over till it's over." - Yogi Berra

Taking time off may be frowned upon, but in all reality, should be encouraged. Players of all ages and at all levels need an offseason; professional players do it, college players do it. It is a necessary break; nonetheless, development shouldn't stop. This time off should give the player a chance to reevaluate their game, mental state towards the game, and overall health.

An athlete playing travel ball year round, playing what seems to be nonstop baseball is a common occurrence, as it is a competitive game in which the race to the top never ends. Though this course has its perks, the downfalls are greater: development is lacking. Development typically only occurs in non-competitive environments, so this time should be taken seriously. Competition is a very important part of the game of baseball, but should not undermine the significance of development.

I am most definitely not discouraging players from playing games, but wish to strongly emphasize the importance of balance between competition and development. If the player is interested in playing another sport, I would encourage them to do this during their "offseason." This allows the body a break from repetitive motions such as throwing and swinging a bat, but is also not harming their athleticism, as they're likely still on their feet, conditioning, and remaining in this positive mindset towards sports.

Another great tool to utilize during this time of development, and even during competition, is video. It acts as a great method to preparation for coming games and practices. Refusing to acknowledge your own weaknesses is a huge weakness in itself; using video to analyze and recognize both strengths and weaknesses in your personal execution of skills is a great step towards overall improvement. Balance, however, also comes into play with this tool: do not analyze it so deeply that it consumes you. The worst thing for an athlete to do is focus on a mistake they made, as they will begin to obsess over it and not be able to overcome it.

I would also like to highlight the importance of mental stimulation. Directly after Game 4 of the 2017 World Series, Clayton Kershaw took the mound at Minute Maid stadium. He did this in a matter of 30 seconds, but stood on the hill, analyzed his surroundings, and eyed each of the bases. This action was all a part of his pregame preparation: knowing he would be pitching Game 5, he wished to truly visualize himself in the position. Kershaw is regarded as one of the most focused and disciplined pitchers in the game at this moment, and this is another prime example as to why. He is so locked on, and so mentally invested in the game that he wakes up, goes to sleep and does everything with the visual of himself performing these skills in game situations.

CHAPTER 6-POST GAME

"There may be people who have more talent than you, but there's no excuse for someone to work harder than you do." -Derek Jeter

The game has ended: your team was victorious; you went 3 for 3, and hit one over. Great. Now what?

Your mind should soon go into post game mode. Ask yourself, "What do I need to do to ensure that I am at the top of my game the next time I step on the field?" On the baseball field, athletes utilize their bodies as machines, executing the same skills repetitively. Aforementioned, a handful of skills rendered while playing baseball aren't natural, meaning that our bodies aren't engineered to do them, let alone tediously. For this reason, the significance of stretching is indescribable. Proper muscle recovery can depend on the muscle, but whether the best method be foam rolling, vascular therapy, simply stretching, or electrical stimulation, I encourage athletes to do it.

Another factor in a player's performance is nutrition. Before, during, and after games, athletes should be sure to put into their body what they expect to get out. As an athlete, it should be kept in mind that more protein and carbohydrates are typically needed than a regular person would need. With this said, the need for fruits, vegetables, and dairy should not be undermined.

On the same note, hydration is also a huge deal for athletes of all sorts. Not only does it affect your overall health, but it also affects your performance. It has been proven that dehydration makes any workout feel harder, and as little as 2% dehydration can cause a drop in endurance. To ensure hydration, aim to drink roughly half of your body weight in ounces of water daily. For example, if you weigh 150 pounds, drink 75 ounces of water daily. This, however, is not a universal principle, as it can vary depending on the individual and their daily activities. Keep in mind that once an active individual feels thirsty, they are already dehydrated.

For optimal performance, I cannot stress how important sleep, on top of nutrition and hydration, is. Vince Lombardi once said, "Fatigue makes cowards of us all." Science backs this statement: Enough sleep is proven to improve reaction times. Low levels of fatigue disable your reaction times by as much, if not more than being legally drunk does. If you wouldn't show up at your game drunk, don't show up to your game tired either. A mind-blowing correlation has also been scientifically proven that your chances of being injured are increased with a lack of sleep. A study looked at high school athletes, and concluded that hours spent in a deep sleep was the strongest predictor of injury. Sleep also affects the mental aspect of the game, as with enough sleep, athletes will likely have fewer mental errors. Sleep deprivation will negatively affect motivation, focus, memory, and learning.

Consider this: A study proved that as the MLB season progressed, players levels of plate discipline decreased, meaning they were swinging at more balls outside of the strike zone at the end of the season than they were at the start. The most logical reason for this trend is the mentally brutal 162 game-long season that results in the player's' mental fatigue.

I am a firm believer in the concept that if an individual doesn't enjoy the sport they are partaking in, their success is highly unlikely. To be successful, an athlete's heart, mind, and body must be passionately devoted to the game. In the services I offer and the athletes I am fortunate enough to train, I aim to implement a go-getter, never-quit, work-harder-than-your-opponent attitude. Simultaneously, I wish to also show each player how

enjoyable the game of baseball is and that their
grand success is possible if they choose to believe
it is and work for it.

CHAPTER 7- CLUBHOUSE TALK

"Actions speak louder than words; let your words teach and your actions speak." - Anthony of Padua

I spoke to Rick's former high school baseball coach, Bob Smith, from Barron Collier, regarding Rick, as well as the relationship he had with his father, Rick Saggese, Sr.

Coach Smith spoke of Rick in extremely high regards. Of all things that Coach Smith had to say about Rick, the denominator in all was that Rick was remarkably dedicated to the game of baseball.

Vividly remembering the first time he met Rick and his father, Coach Smith told me about how when he pulled into the Barron Collier High School parking to see Rick Sr. throwing soft toss and Rick Jr. hitting baseballs into the trunk of their rental car he thought, "Can you believe this?!" From the day they met, Rick continued to illustrate to his varsity baseball coach that he was hard-working, passionate, and above all things, dedicated. Coach Smith explained that Rick was one of the most hard-working players that he coached in all of his 33 years of coaching.

He also explained that Rick was an individual of integrity: He recalls watching him run stadium sprints after practice solely for his own, individual benefit; not to show off, not to brag, but to improve. Coach Smith also recalled Rick taking measures that most high-school kids wouldn't be willing to do, all for baseball. He would put his social life on hold for the sake of the game.

Regarding the relationship that Rick had with his father, Coach Smith said it was one based around support. Rick Sr., in his recall, was a knowledgeable in regards to the game, and would do absolutely anything he could to amplify Rick Jr.'s success.

Coach Smith's closing comments were, "All of his hard work has paid off." Though Rick may not be in the Major Leagues, what he does each and every day is incredible and inspiring. He has built up his knowledge regarding baseball, softball, fitness, and nutrition in such a way that he is a household name in Southwest Florida. Coach Smith said that, undoubtedly, Rick has "earned it himself."

ABOUT THE AUTHOR

Rick played in the Little League World Series after helping his team win on a grand slam to get them to Williamsport, PA.

Rick played his collegiate baseball at the University of Miami; one of the top collegiate baseball programs in the nation. At Miami, Rick battled back from his third knee injury while getting hurt in Honolulu, Hawaii to open the season. He kept his goals in sight once again and became a three-year starter, played in three College World Series, was a Collegiate All-American, and accumulated a career .302 batting average with 21 home runs and 101 RBI's. In 1996 Rick played in the National Championship game against LSU which was arguably the best College World Series title game in history, as LSU won in the ninth inning on a walk off home run. During the 1997 & 1998 summers Rick started for the Hyannis Mets in the Cape Cod Amateur Collegiate Wooden Bat League as he played with and against many players that went on to have successful careers at the Major League level.

Rick is an EXOS Certified Fitness Specialist as well as being certified to perform the Functional Movement Screen (FMS) and Y-Balance Test (YBT). He uses FMS prior to the majority of strength and agility training to assess the athlete for possible for "weak links" associated with their movement patterns. He also not only goes over past injury history with the athlete on the initial session, but does a postural analysis as necessary to find deeper related movement limitations. He has participated in some of the top speed/quickness camps in the country and is a Certified Speed and Agility Coach by the National Sports Performance Association (NSPA). Rick has attended and learned from events taught by various top success and peak performance coaches including Tony Robbins, Dan Lier, and Jim Fannin.

Made in the USA
Columbia, SC
06 March 2023

13010456R00027